# Out of the Ashes of the Ruin

# Out of the Ashes of the Ruin

## A personal testimony

### By

### Lisa Keel Franks

*And they overcame him by the blood of the Lamb and the by the word of their testimony. Revelation 12:11*

authorHOUSE®

AuthorHouse™
1663 Liberty Drive
Bloomington, IN 47403
www.authorhouse.com
Phone: 1 (800) 839-8640

Cover illustrated by Tyler Franks
Edited by Jessica Dellapenta

Published by AuthorHouse  11/19/2015

ISBN: 978-1-5049-6054-0 (sc)
ISBN: 978-1-5049-6053-3 (e)

Library of Congress Control Number: 2015918597

Print information available on the last page.

Any people depicted in stock imagery provided by Thinkstock are models,
and such images are being used for illustrative purposes only.
Certain stock imagery © Thinkstock.

This book is printed on acid-free paper.

# Table of Contents

# A Blessing to My Children

My children,
I did not sit down one day and plan out how to be a mother,
I did not sit down and decide when to be a mother,
Yet, I have always had an innate desire to be a wife and a mother.
Despite my lack of plan, God thought out your very existence
to every hair on your head.
I was not careful of who I would wed.
You all lacked in fatherly advice,
and I tried to play the role once or twice,
but thank God our ears heard the gospel,
and despite our earthly voids we could be full.
Full of the sacrifice of God's own son;
through Him an eternal home is won.
Anchor yourselves in covenant with Him
and you will have a life with no regrets and be filled to the brim.
I am thankful for the Christian line in my family tree.
My prayer for all is to receive the Blessed Assurance of
Heaven where we will be for all eternity.


Love, Mama

# Introduction

In 1 Samuel 30, we see the account of King David and his men returning home to Ziklag:

I Samuel 30:1
"And it came to pass, when David and his men were come to Ziklag on the third day, that the Amalekites had invaded the south and Ziklag, and smitten Ziklag, and burned it with fire…"

I Samuel 30:4
"Then David and the people that were with him lifted up their voice and wept, until they had no more power to weep."

I Samuel 30:8
"And David inquired at the LORD, saying, Shall I pursue after this troop? Shall I overtake them? And he answered him, Pursue: for thou shalt surely overtake them, and without fail recover all."

I Samuel 30:10
"But David pursued, he and four hundred men: for two hundred abode behind, which were so faint that they could not go over the brook Besor."

I Samuel 30:16
"And when he had brought him down, behold, they were spread abroad upon all the earth, eating, and drinking, and dancing, because of all the great spoil that they had taken out of the land of the Philistines, and out of the land of Judah."

I Samuel 30:18
"And David recovered all that the Amalekites had carried away…"

I Samuel 30:23
"Then said David, ye shall not do so, my brethren, with that which the LORD hath given us, who hath preserved us, and delivered the company that came against us into our hand."

I Samuel 30:24
"For who will hearken unto you in this matter? But as his part is that goeth down to the battle, so shall his part be that tarrieth by the stuff…"

This historical event is rich with application to those who have battled the enemy who comes against us "to steal, and to kill, and to destroy" leaving your camp, or your home, in ruin as if burned with fire (John 10:10). We have a spiritual enemy that is mentioned in I Peter 5:8,
"…your adversary the devil, as a roaring lion, walketh about, seeking whom he may devour." In this situation, David

thought things were looking up. He had been living among people that were on his side, they had their own town where family life was good, and he had two wives who respected him (surely his own plan). However, he came home and found everything spoiled; the women and children had been taken and the city burned. As Christ seeks that which is lost, the adversary seeks that which is saved. And he will stop at nothing to have the born again Christian weeping in the ruin with "no more power to weep".

I have been there. According to the standards of the world all was going well in my life, until the enemy saw I had an alliance with God. Then it became war. The only way to survive the battle is to appeal to the LORD God and Jesus Christ our Savior with the goal of redemption for all. One thing of which we can be sure is that the victory has already been won. "O death, where is thy sting? O grave, where is thy victory?" (1 Corinthians 15:55). But thanks be to God who gives us victory through our Lord Jesus Christ! He has finished his work and is sitting at the right hand of God the Father. We can surely overcome through His power that is given to all who believe. Jesus did not leave us comfortless, but the Father sent us the third person of the Godhead, the Holy Spirit, to guide us into remembrance of all things the Word teaches us. However, we have a tendency to grow weary and faint, so we could not make it through the battle without the support of our fellow Christian brothers and sisters (known as the Body) and ministering angels that are provided as a sign of God's love and grace towards us. Notice in 1 Samuel 30 that two hundred were too faint to battle, whereas the enemies spread upon the earth are laughing at what has been spoiled. The fallen angelic spiritual beings are taking joy out of our land and laughing at the harm they bring. Little do they know that our spoils are on the other side. God has preserved us and will deliver us from the enemy's hand.

As you enter the battle "you have to stay by the stuff". You see, David did not have to go into this battle alone. David inquired of the LORD. We inquire of the Lord through the written Word, who became flesh and dwelt among us (John 1:14). As we are crawling in the battle, we are able to endure by the words of scripture which speak to us right where we are. As a parent would not dress their child in a winter parka and gloves in preparation to go to the beach in July, so God the Father would not have us going into battle without being properly equipped. Although He has often given unusual instructions for entering the battle, that is to make it evident that we cannot claim that victory aside from His hand.

Hagar, the bondmaid to Sara, had a wilderness experience. She fled into the wilderness due to the harsh treatment of her mistress after she conceived the child Sara wanted. I see her as a victim of circumstance. The angel of the LORD said to her that the LORD heard her affliction and that she would bear a child. Hagar called on the name of the LORD that day, and He spoke to her in reassurance that everything would be okay: "Your child will be a wild man: his hand will be against every man, and every man's hand against him" (Genesis 16:7-13). It is difficult for me to see how this would have been reassuring for her, but she trusted God that day. She returned to the authority of Sara, but years later was sent away. Abraham sent her out with bread, a bottle of water, and her child, Ishmael. She wandered in the wilderness, and as she lay there facing death, unable to look upon her dying son, the angel of God spoke to her out of heaven. He gave her instructions and opened her eyes to find a well of water. She filled that bottle with water, and the boy grew and survived. Our best made plans to survive and provide leave us with an empty bottle unless we seek the Lord to open our eyes to the spiritual blessings and the water that brings true life. Hagar, living under a righteous man like Abraham, also believed the Word of the LORD concerning the inheritance and blessing of Abraham's seed. She was in covenant as childbearer to the friend of God! She had reassurance that God was with her even though she was enslaved. But the seed of freedom would not come through Ishmael who was birthed out of the flesh's desires and plans, but through Isaac, as God had intended. "Now to Abraham and his seed were the promises made. He saith not, And to seeds, as of many; but as of one, AND TO THY SEED, which is Christ" (Galatians 3:16). Jesus said in a parable to his disciples, "And why call me Lord, Lord, and do not the things which I say? Whosoever comes to me and hears my sayings, and does them, I will show you to whom he is like: He is like a man which built an house, and digged deep, and laid the foundation on a rock: and when the flood rose, the stream beat heavily upon the house, and could not shake it: for it was founded upon a rock. But he that hears and does not, is like a man that without a foundation built a house upon the earth: against which the stream did beat heavily and immediately it fell and the ruin of that house was great" (Luke 6:46-49). We must hear and obey to have our house secure and stable; founded on the Rock, which is Christ.

Part of my desire in writing a portion of my life experiences is to encourage fellow Christian families to "...be strong in the Lord, and in the power of his might" (Ephesians 6:10).

To "Put on the whole armour of God, that ye may be able to stand against the wiles of the devil" (Eph 6:11). And to know that we are wrestling against "...principalities, against powers, against the rulers of the darkness of this world, against spiritual wickedness in high places" (Eph 6:12). We must take to ourselves "the whole armor of God, that we may withstand in the evil day, and having done all, to stand" (Eph 6:13).

This is how we stand: "girded about with truth, having on the breastplate of righteousness, our feet shod with the preparation of the gospel of peace, and above all taking the shield of faith, wherewith ye shall be able to quench all the fiery darts of the wicked. And take the helmet of salvation, And the sword of the Spirit, which is the Word of God: Praying always with all prayer and supplication in the Spirit and watching with all perseverance and supplication for all saints: As for me, that utterance may be given unto me that I may open my mouth boldly, to make known the mystery of the gospel. For which I am an ambassador in bonds" (Eph 6:14-20). Let us dig deep and build on the foundation of Christ so that our House will stand.

Jesus fulfilled the prophetic words of Isaiah as Christ himself stood up in the synagogue and read from Isaiah 61:14, "The spirit of the Lord God is upon me; because the LORD hath anointed me to preach good tidings unto the meek; he hath sent me to bind up the brokenhearted, to proclaim liberty to the captives, and the opening of the prison to them that are bound; To proclaim the acceptable year of the LORD, and the day of vengeance of our God; to comfort all that mourn; To appoint unto them that mourn in Zion, to give unto them beauty for ashes, the oil of joy for mourning, the garment of praise for the spirit of heaviness, that they might be called trees of righteousness, the planting of the LORD, that he might be glorified. And they shall build the old wastes, they shall raise up the former desolations, and they shall repair the waste cities, the desolations of many generations."

Isaiah, a prophet for God, spoke of the promise of the seed which would come. The seed came in the form of Jesus, who was born of a virgin woman. He left us with the seed of His person, the Holy Spirit. We, as the children of God, are anointed with an "unction" for His call and purpose (2 John 2:20). Being in Christ, the Spirit of the Lord is upon us to preach good tidings which liberate those that are brokenhearted and bound. I don't want to just learn how to stand for my benefit, I want to share the good news. Let me share my journey on how the Lord transformed my ashes into beauty.

*God, I acknowledge You.*
*I am so amazed at your creations.*
*How you thought us into existence down to the very cells, the very hairs on our head. Our minds, they are limited.*
*Our bodies, so reliant.*
*Our souls need to be full of compassion as your Son demonstrated.*
*Our hearts are prone to wander.*
*Our strength is in You.*

*I am amazed at our family heritage.*
*I am so thankful for my family tree being engrafted to You and Your Son, Jesus.*
*I am thankful for being linked to Christians who show a love for family and live a holy, sacrificial life.*

*I pray my life honestly and sincerely displays Christ and the Word of God through my actions. First and foremost, living a healthy life of forgiveness, and leading others to have a personal relationship with You;*

*Lisa Keel Franks*

*A relationship unshaken and sure through all eternity.*

*I acknowledge that I am chosen by Him for a special purpose, which is to live in covenant with Him; therefore, I will give to Him a life that lifts up His Holy name and praises Him as my God.*

*Your daughter*

# CHAPTER ONE

# My Testimony

When I was asked to speak to the Ladies Auxiliary in August 2005, I began to think about how to summarize my testimony that proclaims the truths of the gospel while sharing my witness to the power of these truths through my own personal experiences. I believe every person has a story and Jesus shed his blood for the remission of sin to cover many.

"This is my story; this is my song; praising my Savior all the day long…" was a song heard often in my grandmother Keel's church on weekend visits to Gold Point, NC (Crosby and Knapp). Let me go back a bit to tell you about my story. My dad, James Keel, was raised during The Great Depression and was the middle child of nine children. Now, whenever I hear a reference to a fine, grayhaired, godly saint of a woman, I imagine his mother. I did not entirely understand what made her so precious until my own eyes were opened to the spiritual things of the Lord.

My mother, Ann Stokes, was one of five girls who were also raised by a Christian mother. Baba Stokes passed away when I was seven, so I don't remember much about her, but I have had the privilege to look through some of her notes with my Aunt Betsy (also a lovely Christian) that she wrote when she was young. The evidence of her love for God was expressed in writing.

September 19, 1912
Sixteenth Birthday

> Thank God for the one who is cheerful,
> In spite of life's troubles, I say
> Who sings of a brighter tomorrow
> Because of the clouds of today
> His life is a beautiful sermon and
> This is the lesson to me
> Meet trials with smiles and they vanish,
> Face cares with a song and they flee
> (Author Uncertain)

As I reflect over my family tree full of righteous fruit, I think about the struggles encountered among the first chosen Hebrew family. May the life of Lot, the son of Abraham's brother, serve as a lesson in a family lineage. Even though Lot was considered righteous, he was vexed of no witness to others in the city; his words meant nothing to his family when they stood at the brink of judgment. 2 Peter 2:7 says God "...delivered just [righteous] Lot, vexed [troubled or greatly distressed] with the filthy conversations of the wicked." Lot looked to the richest field of the land when Abraham offered to separate due to the immensity of their family and belongings. His choice caused him some troubles at the time, and when God appointed the final judgment of the city, it cost him his family, friends, and community, with the exception of two virgin daughters. Abraham was counted righteous because he sojourned by faith at the voice of God, yet he navigated off course a few times as well. We have an obligation to continue the knowledge and truth of a relationship in Christ from generation to generation so as not to lose even one family member to the wickedness of this current world in which we live.

***The Keel Family, Mama and Dad
far right, Grandma center***

### *The Stokes Family, Grandma far left, Mama far right*

As a child, I was "brought up" in church. Myself and two older brothers, Alan and Stuart, were raised by our Dad. Our mother left when we were young. That was the beginning of the enemy attack. I bet the devils were laughing over that one, But GOD was still in control. I gained another biological brother, Shawn, when Mama remarried. My mother made Florida their home and we had visitation one month of every summer. I will say she did try to give us a great vacation every year. I loved the sun and water. I have fond memories of our visits to see Mama's sisters and our cousins whenever she traveled to NC. In my adult years, I realize how blessed I am with the double connection with my blood relatives and our Kingdom connection in Christ. Shawn and I have grown very close as we grew older. We *all* had our trials to face and we discovered over time who had the power to help us.

**Me and Shawn**

My Daddy remarried when I was nine for a brief four years. Through this, I gained my step sister Tracy, whom I would not have known otherwise, and we love each other as if we were blood related. She was five years old at the time, and her brother Gary was even younger. Our home was unsettled during those four years. I remember trying to read the bible for comfort at ten years old and not understanding the long genealogies of the "begats". I ended up putting it aside. My Dad continued in the same church during this time, but I lost interest at the age of fourteen, having been drawn away by the interests of the world. My group of friends were not attending. I also believe I was impacted by the details shared with me at this age about the events of my parents separation. No one in the church, my parents, or their siblings had ever talked about it. In hindsight, I believe the news moved me in a direction away from the church.

I had a wonderful earthly father who made me feel secure (plus two protective older brothers), especially with troubling situations. I'll confess the troubles were created by my own choices. I knew that he would be there for me. After all, he had not forsaken us or left us seeking bread. He helped me out financially on many levels. Despite this security, there were things I was ashamed to take before my earthly father. Instead, I would seek God with my list of problems, all the while sensing He did exist. That was all I knew on a spiritual level from my childhood experience in church.

I mainly prayed to God when I was afraid or worried. When I got my driver's license in 1979, I remember asking God to help me get home safe while driving impaired. I promised I would never do it again. Later, I was actually stopped by an officer and asked to do a sobriety test. When asked for my license, I handed him my Athens Drive student ID instead. I was dismissed; I suspected the officer knew my Dad. Why else would he let me go? I remembered turning to God again when I needed to pass the nursing boards. I had just turned twenty years old, was pregnant with Shane and had married his Dad because of the pregnancy. "I need the job to take care of this baby," I told God. And I passed.

As for relationships, I suppose the nurse in me looked for men who needed my help-men that I could nurture. I had a strong desire to marry and have a family at a young age. I had been the "little mother" taking care of the house chores and trying to cook for my Dad and brothers. My first marriage lasted long enough to have two children in three years. I found myself in a very stressful environment greatly influenced by alcohol. I had four children to provide for: two stepsons, Teddy and Timmy (then 7 and 5 years old), and my two babies, Shane and Jessica, who were eleven months apart. Tough days starting out in which I refrain from giving details. I remember the time I looked in the refrigerator to find only one egg and a bottle of Hershey's chocolate syrup. Again, Daddy never left us begging for bread. I often ran to him. I loved these children so much, I wanted to keep us together. Timmy seemed to miss his Mom but they were loyal to me in their young age. For safety reasons, I fled to Florida to live with my mother for a year in 1987. I asked to have custody of Teddy and Timmy, but was not allowed. Turns out their grandparents, Jackie and Bob, kept the boys. Aunt Liz was with them or at least nearby. After things began to settle down from what seemed like a nightmare, I moved back home to North Carolina. Eventually, Teddy and Timmy moved back with their Mom when they became teenagers. I tried to get the boys back here for a visit but it never seemed to work out. Unfortunately, harsh tragedy struck us as Teddy and Timmy left this world at the young ages of 25 and 27. On Thanksgiving Day of 2002 they were in a car accident as they traveled to their mom's home in Connecticut to have a family meal together. I will never forget that phone call when their Dad contacted me, we were celebrating our traditional Keel Family Reunion having our meal of Thanksgiving together. Through Christ's love we are all at peace with each other to this day.

### *Teddy, Jessica, Shane and Timmy*

I began to seek a church for myself and children. I usually worried about my children's ability to sit still in church, afraid they would bother someone. Shane and Jessica were preschoolers at the time and were actually very well behaved. For a time the enemy used my worries to distract me and hinder my knowledge and understanding of the gospel. I gave up for a few years. Later, as I was visiting Midway Baptist Church, I met Jonathan Franks, he lived at the end of my street. We began to date. We were both 25 years old, with his son Jay and my daughter Jessica both being 5 years old, and my son Shane was 6 years old. I learned that Jonathan had been raised in that church. I thought I had found a sincere, nice young man one you can bring home to introduce to your parents! Soon after, he wanted to visit other churches, but we ended up not attending church altogether. I was working twelve hour shifts every other weekend. We were cohabiting, as he had rented out his home and moved in with me. I developed a bond with Jay, that has lasted to this day. I was regularly picking him up from school for Jonathan's visitation times. I often had to go find him on the school playground or in the classroom. We had quality time in the car ride. Jay was easy to get to know, he can talk with anyone.

I was in love. Life was routine and simple around our house. About 18 months later, I became pregnant with Tyler. We decided we needed more space. I was working one weekend and asked my patient if I could look at the classified section of his newspaper because I was looking for land. His visitor, who happened to be a preacher, told me of some land for sale around McGee's Crossroads. We pursued this and purchased the land where we resided for the next fourteen years. We were married on September 22, 1991. I look back on that and realize that God placed us here to receive the spiritual strength that I would need for the battles to come.

**Mr. and Mrs. Franks, Shane, Jessica, Jay in front**

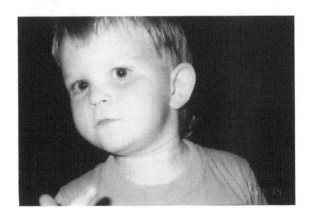

**Tyler**

Jonathan and I suggested going to church on Easter and Christmas. We sat in the back row pew of a nearby church.

The pastor's message included a story about a young man who had just died in a car accident whom he had been trying to "win" for Christ. The man resisted, and now all he could do was stand at his grave. That stuck with me, but I was confused by the worship of speaking in tongues openly since I had never been exposed to it, so I never went back. I didn't have the Holy Spirit to help me understand any of this at the time.

Four months later, I flipped and rolled my car across I40 with my three children. None of us were restrained except for Tyler in the baby car seat. Which was in the front seat, facing forward. I felt the presence of guardian angels turn that car right side up as we landed in safety. Every single window was completely shattered except the side window Jessica had her head rested against. Tyler's infant cries sounded like he went out the window, but he was still in his seat covered in glass without a scratch on him. Shane was stretched out asleep on the back seat before he was rudely awakened. Actually, we had all been asleep. I was very sleep deprived during this time. Little did I know how dead I was spiritually in my trespasses. I was more convinced that the LORD God wanted my attention.

Wow! Look how God was preserving his children from injury for His appointed work to be accomplished in the future. I thought about this as compared to Jacob, the son of Isaac. Rachel inquired of the Lord as to the twins' war in her womb, and before he was even born, it was spoken of what kind of leader Jacob would be. He went on to wrestle with God after many disappointments in his life.and received the blessing that he would be called Israel, representing the twelve tribes of the chosen people. We were preserved to be Ambassadors for Christ in our small corner of the world, or wherever He chooses to send us. He was blessing my family with safety before we even knew Him.

We went back to visiting churches but could not find a connection. I was looking for children that were my children's age to make church more enticing to them. One cold January day, a visitor came to our house to invite our family to church. Jonathan was working on the well and troubleshooting problems with the water. This visitor, Thurman McLamb, got involved. He went home to get his tools and stood out there in the 17 degree weather helping Jonathan. We all got a laugh when we realized three hours later the water hose was left running under the house. Shane had given the dog's water. This act of kindness led us to visit Friendship Baptist Church. We began to attend regularly but not faithfully. I heard the gospel preached for the first time through my pastor, Brother Mack Fowler. I had never realized what God's own son had done for me, nor the significance of his anointed blood that was shed. At this time, I was the happiest I had ever been. I had my husband whom I loved, my children, and a nursing career. However, it wasn't until four years later that I was confronted by my sinful nature, how ignorantly I had lived all those years. I was godly sorrowful unto tears in a revival that was held March of 1998 by Brother Teague Groves. I realized that I was in need of a Savior, a Lord. "But when it pleased God, who separated me from my mother's womb, and called me by his grace, to reveal his Son in me..." (Galatians 1:15-16). The person of the Holy Spirit drew me and opened my eyes to the areas of my guilt and my transgressions against a Holy God who is the creator of all.

Six months later, the revival was held again by the same preacher and my brother Alan was saved by his confession of Christ. He would go on to marry Mary, a wonderful

Christian woman from a great family of believers. They were blessed with two sons named John and Aaron, along with Alan's oldest son, Brandon. They truly are the kindest family unit I know. They give freely out of their blessings. They have allowed me to bring guests to their home with no questions asked. Their response is *always* "come on". One time I arrived with three young children on a weekend getaway to their home at the beach, I was trying to take the children's mind off their mother being incarcerated. My brother Alan put a "Keel" baseball uniform on the middle child and allowed him to play in the opening scrimmage baseball game with his son Aaron's team. The boy was nine years old and had never been given that opportunity, actually never played baseball. I could go on and on with examples. Tyler and his friends, and all my children have been blessed with many fishing trips on "Reel Faith" charters, and enjoying the atmosphere of their home.

**Tyler, Ridge, Collin, John**

You know the devil did not mind all those years I believed in God, for even the devils believe. As a matter of fact, they know of His existence because they are His creation also, but they were rebellious and cast out (Revelation 12:9). The enemy knew I was still lost in this world that belongs to him. It was at the time of my true salvation that Satan began his work to knock our feet right out from under us by taking out the head of the household. I believe when "Mama got saved", our children took notice. Jonathan had a confession of faith from his youth.

Concerns had already started to surface, but much to my surprise, Jonathan agreed that we would never have alcohol in our house again. We threw out the alcohol that used to be acceptable on our Friday night of "unwinding" from a stressful week. Yet, a problem increased in another area. By January 1999, I was looking at it head on. Nine months after our whole family had been baptized, I realized my husband was under a stronghold leading him away. It had been a slow fade that was now in full flight away from our once happy home. I took on full responsibility to provide for the children. Matter of fact, he was working against me concerning money. I was often left without transportation for two or three days at a time. One Christmas Eve, he disappeared with all the children's presents in the trunk of the car. Praise God that his brother Barry drove me around until we found our car. In times past, when I would get out of my bed to go looking for him, I could never find him. The pressure was mounting, so I sought help to discuss it with a counselor through the Employee Assistance Program at my work. The counselor described me as a little child in front of a big wall where the dam is threatening to break. With each hole that popped up, I would run to put my hand over it. I was running myself crazy in an attempt to cover up the problems.

I did not want the Christians of the church to know what was going on in my home. I was a babe in Christ, but I held on to verses in the scripture for strength. "What God hath joined together, let no man put asunder" (Matthew 19:6). I sat in church many Sundays hiding my tears and the shame of the true condition of my household. Christians often wear a mask to say everything is great. I had resorted to what I knew as a teenage sinner: hiding the things that I was too ashamed to confess and trying to cover them up. It is the nature of our flesh and confusion. We see this example in Adam and Eve's first efforts to run from God and hide from their sin and shame. I saw the truth that God had to cover their sin and mine with the shedding of blood in which Jesus came and shed his blood to cover us once and for all. Knowing Jesus changed how I prayed to God as the trials and attacks continued. I was learning His Word as my guide and defense.

I would get really angry in response to Jonathan's choices. I would be upset and burdened down after an incident. Very oddly, the burden and anger would lift by the third day of spending time in the scriptures. I spent one weekend reading the entire book of Job while feeling the burden from the enemy. I gained a tremendous lesson from Job 42:5, "I have heard of thee by the hearing of the ear: but now mine eye sees thee." At the end of Job's trial, he knew God with an intimacy that he had never known before. I gained strength by reading God's Word. I could hold on to small truths such as, "I'm kept by the Lord" (John 17:12); "by faith into the grace wherein we stand" (Romans 5:2); "when you've done all you can do, just stand" (Ephesians 6:13). I struggled with scripture that gave directives such as "wives be submissive to your husband..." (Colossians 3:18). Then I would justify myself by summarizing that this is in reference to a righteous man! I wanted to take scripture and recite it to Jonathan to "fix" him with God's Word or to help him see his wrongs. I had found the cure and I wanted to force him to eat and drink of it. I was actually forcing his free will. I would give it to him directly:

"For let not that wavering man think that he shall receive anything of the Lord." James 1:7

"Ye are of your father, the devil, and the lusts of your father ye will do. He was a murderer from the beginning and abode not in the truth, because there is no truth in him." John 8:44

"Ye cannot drink the cup of the Lord and the cup of devils: man cannot partake of the Lord's table and of the table of devils." 1 Corinthians 10:21

I was still an immature Christian using the sword inappropriately in the battle. However, Jesus put the soldier's ear back on after Peter went slashing. The scripture came and guided me: "...deliver such a one unto Satan for the destruction of the flesh, that the spirit may be saved in the day of the Lord Jesus" (I Corinthians 5:5). I asked Jonathan to leave in the fall of 1999. He returned back home after three months, but within one week the same problem resurfaced. I kept trying to make it work until February 2001.

I was visiting my brother Stuart's home, and a young seventeen-year-old boy was also staying there while his foster parents were on vacation. He was orphaned at the age of nine when their home burned down while he and his mom were sleeping. His older sister was a friend of my sister-in-law, Angie. Stuart and Angie have opened their home many times to those who were hurting or in need. We were outside by the pool, talking about the things of the Lord. He told me he felt the gift of prophecy upon his life. He said, "Right now, I see you burdened down with stress, and I do not even recall what this verse says, but God is telling me to tell you to read Jeremiah 29:11-13." Don't you know I ran through that house with water dripping in my path as I went to open my bible. "For I know the thoughts I have toward you, says the LORD, thoughts of peace, not of evil, to bring you to an expected end. Then shall you call upon me, and ye shall go and pray unto me and I will hearken unto you. And ye shall seek me and find me, when ye shall search for me with all of your heart." I was bubbling with joy because I needed to take my focus off Jonathan. Jonathan and I went on to live apart for two and a half years. We planned to reconcile when he could prove his sincerity and take care of our family.

At the time of Jonathan's departure from our home, I was involved with Children's Church on Wednesday nights. Tyler was eight years old at the time. I made a dedication to serve at the church by getting involved with the Vacation Bible School the summer of 2000. I also became involved in Precept Bible Studies with my friend Heidi Massey when I saw how she was learning to study the bible inductively. When you love the Lord, you will feel a burning desire to help in some capacity in the church or community. I was growing in His Word and becoming stronger in my faith. You need His Word for fuel to energize you and give you wisdom to share with others. God laid a concern on my heart that the youth needed more time in the Word on their level of understanding. There was no special service offered above the age of eleven, which meant they would then go in the regular services with the adults. The Lord led me to extend the opportunity for that age group to have their own gathering place in the church. I knew this directive was not only for my own son's benefit, but also because we as a church body have a responsibility to our younger generation. It was a really cool time as Tyler brought in his friends. I purchased a vehicle with them in mind to accommodate transportation as Tyler had 3-4 friends willing to come every Wednesday night. We had the basement as our space and the early teens came to socialize and skateboard as they heard the gospel taught.

In the Spring of 2002, I was studying the book of James through the Precept Ministry and felt James 5:20 come to life regarding my current situation with Jonathan: "Let him know, that he which converteth the sinner from the error of his way, shall save a soul from death and shall hide a multitude of sins." I found Jonathan in a most pitiful condition. I spoke with him and encouraged him to seek professional help, promising that I would take him back and support him in any way I could. Finding an affordable arrangement was difficult, but he agreed to an inpatient center for twenty one days. I agreed to live with him again on his return to his aunt's house where he was renting. For the next year Tyler and I lived with him, and he remained in a good spiritual condition with love and support from the church and his family for the first seven months. He was full of passion towards worship and church service. He was bold in terms of speaking to strangers or anyone to convince them of a relationship with Christ. He was leading the household and doing well to provide for us.

Immediately after a phone call from his "friend", whom he had met in the group program, I noticed a change, he lost his focus. The friend stated that she was having trouble finding a support group that she could connect with since departure and wanted to talk with Jonathan.

Contact with her was a turning point; he began hiding his phone calls and his location, and strange people began to show up in the driveway asking for him. I remember the stray shepherd we had taken in, you could tell he was police trained. He would not allow one particular man to get out of his car when he drove up. He was barking in his face to the point that Tyler and I could not make out what he was saying other than that he was asking for Jonathan. He got frustrated and drove off. Tyler and I went inside and proceeded to have our first powerful prayer together, pleading the blood of Jesus over the doorposts so that the enemy could not come there. I had spent much effort declaring to the devil, "you will not have my husband!" I could not believe that Jonathan's tears, profession of faith, and love for Jesus were anything but sincere. He spoke so boldly, proclaiming Jesus is the only way. I stayed another five months waiting to see what decisions he would make to correct things, and it just got worse. He would disappear for three days at the time. I was literally praying for God to take him, saying to God in my anguish, "See, he isn't going to serve you!" Selfish I know. I was focused on myself and a broken covenant, feeling that I was never going to have the spiritual leader I truly did need-not even thinking of what Tyler was losing in a father.

I was again facing shattered dreams. I had pictured Jonathan and myself moving forward in ministry together. I thought we would partner together to help many young people make better choices than we had made in our youth: How to choose to have a relationship with Jesus at an early age and avoid the pain we suffered from our choices to have a life without regrets. What could I do but to keep pressing "toward the mark for the prize of the high calling of God in Christ Jesus" (Philippians 3:14) one of Tyler's favorite scriptures at this age.

How did He guide me?

By keeping my eyes on Jesus and seeing Him high and lifted up.

By giving me encouraging words from my Christian friends. Through sitting under Spiritled messages.

By revealing truths to me through His Word, helping me to share these with those who would listen, and giving me guidance in how to apply these truths to my life.

I had put my heartache into words Christmas of 2001:

Happy Birthday, Jesus: To My Husband

God in His infinite wisdom and power
planned to the very hour,
when he would send His son
for our salvation the victory through flesh he won.

His plan of Grace laid out before the foundation of the earth,
that God would offer every soul through Jesus' birth,
to establish unto Him a Kingdom and Government, to rule
with justice and pure judgment.

He left his position above the angels in heaven,
and walked among us as the Word unleavened.
His heart's desire to do his Father's will
being mocked, rejected, tormented, then killed.

Through the Resurrection the Victory was displayed,
that Jesus is the Truth, the Life, the Way.

His light shines in the dark place
For ALL to seek the Master's face.

Tell me true,
what part of God's perfect plan failed for you?
what area did he leave undone,
leaving you seeking a darkness you will not shun?

None are perfect; no not one.
For His Mercy is great that he extends upon.
For myself, I long to understand what prompts you to lose
His hand.

God knows your heart; he knew before you were born.
He knows where you struggle and where you are torn.
As for myself, I will continue to pray
For your safe return from the evil spirit that leads you astray.

I stand firm in Hope that the natural eye cannot see,
that from my husband's bondage on his soul he will be set
free. That in His love our family can be joined together
where we will Glorify our God forever and ever.

"That was the true light, which lighteth every man that
cometh into the world." John 1:9

# CHAPTER TWO

# Serving Through the Pain

Summer of 2003, I sat in a lawyer's office and drew up separation papers to protect myself financially from Jonathan's choices. I told him my situation, and he paused, looked at me, and said, "After all you have been through, you only have this amount of outstanding debt?" I attributed my position to having a wonderful father, but I should have shared with him that my heart was warmed not just by the earthly one. I give God the glory for his provision and grace on us.

I announced by way of letter to the deacons of my church my intention to divorce Jonathan. I expressed that I understood if they would rather I not teach or lead. However, the church did not consider me unworthy to lead, so I did not stop serving.

The Lord was helping me to look at myself, to examine areas of weakness and recognize that I needed lots of refining, and that I was just at risk of stumbling. As Galatians 5:17 indicates, our flesh is against the Spirit and hinders us from the things we should do. I felt lonely and disappointed as I glanced back over my life. I felt the impact of wanting to see the light of my dreams come true.

Who knew God was planning to raise up Tyler to be called with a special purpose? Not only Tyler, but Shane would become a mighty voice for God, and my daughter a mighty prayer warrior. I can so relate to Sara as she waited on the promise of a seed, but in desperation created an Ishmael. Her actions delayed God's plan. He had to wait until Ishmael was of an age to be moved on before the seed could be birthed. In other words, we can abort or delay what God wants to birth when we take our own actions. I have been guilty of this many times. We have to hold fast to our promises and wait. The beauty of this is that Hebrews 11:11 tells us "Sara received strength to conceive seed, and was delivered of a child when she was past age, because she judged him faithful who had promised." I love this chapter that displays the faith of God's people. Despite ourselves and the error of our ways, our faith leads us to His glory. Therein lies our hope.

Let's take a moment to gain insight by looking over Abraham's walk with God. After all, the LORD said, "... in thee all families of the earth will be blessed" (Genesis 12:3). When Abram was told by God to leave his country because He would show him a land, he did. Although he did not know where he was going, he left with his father and his brother's son, Lot, whom he probably loved as a son. First, he went to Haran until his father died, then on toward Canaan. He *passed through* Shechem, and the Lord appeared to reinforce His promise that He would give his seed this land. Abram's response was to *move* toward Bethel. **He called upon the name of the LORD and built an altar.** He then *moved* toward Egypt (south Negev) in fear of his life. He made the decision to lie, and could have possibly lost the promise of a seed had his wife been kept by Pharaoh. God had to intervene to ensure that Pharaoh discovered the truth. Abram journeyed back to Bethel (translated: the house of God), which is where he had pitched his tent at the place of the altar and the place where he had called upon the name of the LORD.

The bible states the land could not support all their possessions, and there was dissension among the herders, so Lot departed to his choice of land. God then spoke to Abram: "For all the land which thou seest, to thee I will give it, and thy seed forever" (Genesis 13:15). At the Lord's direction, Abram roamed through the land that he was to receive. He moved his tent to Hebron and built an altar unto the LORD.

He had dwelt there ten years when Sara decided to use her Egyptian handmaid (when they were sent away by the Pharaoh they were given maidservants) to be a surrogate mother for her. Sara later dealt harshly with Hagar and she fled. Sometimes our circumstances seem too harsh and we want to run from them. The angel of the LORD found her by a fountain of water in the wilderness, by the fountain on the way to Shur, and gave her instructions and a blessing. She knew the LORD saw her and would provide for her. The well of water was called Beer Lahai Roi, meaning "the well of the Living One." We can know God does see us in our circumstance of pain.

The life lesson that I see through Abraham's journey was that he was willing to sacrifice, and he moved in obedience. In instances of fear, and later a lack of patience, he took some wrong steps, but the LORD was faithful in rescuing him and allowing him to come back to worship and serve as the chosen Hebrew. The LORD made a covenant with him and changed his name from Abram to Abraham.

Hebrews 11:13-16 *(New American Standard Bible)* states: "All these died in faith, without receiving the promises, but having seen them and having welcomed them from a distance, and having confessed that they were strangers and exiles on the earth. For those who say such things make it clear that they are seeking a country of their own. And indeed if they had been thinking of that country from which they went out, they would have had opportunity to return. But as it is, they desire a better country, that is a heavenly one. Therefore God is not ashamed to be called their God: for He has prepared a city for them." Blessings because of one man's obedience. We all have potential to make poor choices that lead us off God's chosen path, but He can redirect our footsteps. Life apart from God is not worth going back to.

This stage of spiritual battle drew near an end as Jonathan carried on with his life. In mid-October of 2005, he called me at 2 o'clock in the morning to apologize for all he put me through because now he knew firsthand how I felt. I told him that I did not know how, but if he was willing to serve God one hundred percent, we would work through this problem and serve the Lord together. If God was working, I did not want to miss it. I felt the sacrifice of Isaac; just as he did not resist his father who bound him and placed him on the altar, so I was willing to lay myself aside. Isaac was a grown man when he went up that mountain with Abraham, and he knew there was something very important missing from their planned sacrifice. He said to his Father, "I see the wood, and I see the fire, but where is the Lamb?" (Genesis 22:7). We cannot see all with the natural eye. We have to look for the Lord to provide. But he did not respond to my offer. It is hard to say if this was of God or of me who wanted so desperately to have him back. Now, I personally could not see any more hope. I drew the conclusion that I was scripturally released. The fall of this same year, David asked me out again for a date. I had come to his house to borrow tools I needed for various jobs to repair the home that I was fixing up to sell. We had been neighbors for fifteen years. His wife left their relationship in 2001, the same year I had Jonathan removed from our home. I thought that this was some sort of spiritual connection between us. I had avoided the invitation to go out to the movies or dinner on two previous occasions, but now that Jonathan had made his choice, I agreed to go with David to Mule Days in Benson to see the rodeo. I had lived in this county all this time and had never gone to this event. He started calling me to go out every other weekend when he didn't have his son staying with him. As we began dating, I needed to know whether David was a believer. That is an important question. He explained that they didn't go to church as a family because it was the least path of resistance during that time. He said he accepted Christ at the young age of fifteen years old. Well, that was all I needed to hear, right?

I had set a goal in my heart not to remarry until Tyler was eighteen. All of our children had been through so much. However, the temptations were great. I told David I did want not to sin against God. Remember, I was pregnant in a wedding dress twice before. I was a new creature in Christ and the old way was not acceptable. He respected the Word of God on that issue. I so admired him for waiting. I had respect for the man I saw in him, his dedication to his children and his surviving father. He impressed me that he was always available to his family and they were his priority. He shared with me by December of 2005 that he was in love with me. However, I was not divorced yet and still the wife of Jonathan. (In hindsight, I was wrong to be dating). On my birthday, he proposed to marry me after discussing his desire with Tyler, Jessica and his two children.

He didn't ask Shane, and I wasn't willing to listen to Shane while he was objecting. We wed September 2006, with the understanding that we would maintain two households for the benefit of our children. At what point did I build an altar and ask God? It was more like, "Yes" everything feels right, we have fun together, and we have the same concerns for our children's well being. And I was having the most fun in our travels, long road trips on David's Road King, riding dirt bikes and ATV's in the West Virginia "hollows" was more beautiful than Disney. We had a lot of laughs as David taught me to ride the dirt bike. He was so patient with me as I tore things up. I started having "fun" at the age of 40, I learned to snow ski with Tyler on special trips to Ohio with my cousin Debra and her husband Michael. Now, David and his son and daughter joined in learning to ski. All the emotions of fun, for a season. I remember in the early stages of dating, when we stayed on the phone for hours and didn't consider the difficulty of working with only a few hours of sleep, like teenagers in our forties. I told David I had no idea what the Lord would have me to do it may be mission work out of the country. I did not know, but I felt in my spirit that I would serve in any capacity the Lord directed. I was feeling something, as if I needed to warn him before we went any further in our relationship.

In January 2007 we began to worship at Lighthouse Baptist Church as a family. We had need to come together in our worship. David had visited Lighthouse with his daughter, and although I was still serving at Friendship, I was resigned to go where my husband was led. Not long after becoming part of the family at Lighthouse, an opportunity was given to join a mission trip to Costa Rica. We were to complete a servant team of fourteen to sixteen people with the first international In His Wakes water sports ministry.

The Spirit was drawing me to join this team. I convinced David that the financial support would come in, so there would be no burden for us to get involved. He agreed to join.

It was an awesome experience, and it was amazing to watch God work and meet every need. Nate, the leader of In His Wakes, arrived a week ahead of the team to visit the surrounding villages and invite the children for "A Day 2 Remember". Many of the locals in this area were immigrants from Nicaragua and were not allowed to attend school. They were given the opportunity to learn how to ski with the team of professional water skiers while the caimans laid on the bank of the waters. Many of the young children were just as excited to have the peanut butter sandwich we provided at lunch because they had no food for breakfast. We were set up for thirty, but seventy showed up. At the end of the day, Nate gave a message to illustrate the boat represents God with Jesus being the rope. You have to chose to hold on to Jesus to be connected to the power source. We were so blessed to be a part of His work. Just prior to this trip though, I began to recognize problems entering our marriage. Trying to bring two families together created a wedge that would keep us from ever being one.

# CHAPTER THREE

## Tyler's Eyes Opened

This same month of March 2008, my eyes were opened to the devil's tactics against my youngest one in the garden. The mischief the boys had been getting into was finally brought to my attention by the parents of Tyler's friends. After my emotions calmed down, the Lord led me on what to say to our child. I asked Tyler to explain to me what life was like in the garden for Adam. I told him that his driver's license was a privilege and that because of his decisions the pleasures of the garden were gone. As another consequence, he would now have to labor as Adam did. We reviewed the consequences of Adam, Eve, and the serpent, and talked about how Eve was beguiled by the serpent. Tyler proceeded to ask me, "Is it really a sin to…? My friends and I searched the Bible and we did not find any mention of it, so we thought it must be alright." Then the eyes were opened! "Oh, son, don't you see how Satan beguiled you by asking you 'what does God's Word say about…'?"

My daughter Jessica was home and came to join us in the revelation. She shared that knowing her father was a heavy drinker, she made a decision to not use any substances for fear of it leading to a stronghold over her life. We hit the altar in the middle of our living room and prayed that we would resist the wiles of the enemy. Tyler hopped up and ran up the street to share the insight with his friend. When you have been with God, you will run to tell someone.

Tyler was a sixteen-year-old looking for a job, and at this time in his life he began to question the future and whether he would attend college. I was doing my bible study one Saturday morning in May, two months after the revelation of the boys' mischief. Tyler still had too much time on his hands to play since he had yet to find a job. I took a quick break in my study and my thoughts of worry went to Tyler and what he would do. God spoke in my subconscious, "He is going to be a pastor." I was clearly hearing this and it was not of my own imagination. So, I decided I would share this with him. He responded, "I know. He has been dealing with me also." The word was out and the devil got busier.

More time spent with his friends led to more mischief, but this time the Lord was leading me to see things that were going on rather than being blindsided with the reports from my neighbors. Well, actually, there were still a few calls from the neighbors that took me by surprise! I would explain to Tyler that God was leading me to see things in order to keep him on the right path and that God had a plan for him.

July 21st of this same year, Tyler went to a Youth Alive event in Tennessee. The Saturday night before his departure, God spoke to me again during my bible study time and told me to ask Tyler if he loves Him, as Jesus asked Peter in John 21. Tyler came into my room and we sat face to face. I asked him the questions God had directed me to ask him, saying, "God wants to know if you love Him." I asked him three times, just as Peter was asked. With each of his replies, I responded as Jesus did: "...feed my lambs...feed my sheep" (John 21:15-16). The call was to pastor over the sheep. With each time I repeated the question, I saw the grief on Tyler's face, the same as Peter probably felt when Jesus had to hear his commitment three times.

At the opening service of the event in Tennessee, the leader asked the crowd of 1,700 teenagers if God had spoken to any of them to lead as a pastor, and if so, to stand to their feet and go back home and tell their church what God was calling them to do so their church could support them. So he did. I was indescribably blessed to see him in the Word without having to bribe him with treats or money like I used to do to motivate the youth group. He was asking for knowledge from God to understand what he read. He explained to me that his first baptism at the age of six was not sufficient. God had lead him through Proverbs for wisdom, and he would leave me notes about new things in the Word coming to life for him. He began to get involved in the activities of Vacation Bible School at Lighthouse. He was given the opportunity to join the Praise team and use his gift of playing guitar. He also benefited by learning more about music as he served. It was a blessing that our music director, John Creech, was willing to work with him. I was so excited to have my child as a fellow laborer for Christ. I began to get a glimpse that God was comforting me from the spiritual battle with Tyler's Dad. Tyler was appointed, but was now in much need of prayer to resist the devil, who seeks to devour his efforts to further the gospel.

He had never expressed any interest in attending college. With this call in mind, he decided that since man requires it, he would go talk to the student counselor for guidance. Tyler set up an appointment, and as he walked in the door she said, "I've got it all figured out, Tyler you should go to Appalachian State for construction management." She made that assumption based on the electives he had taken.

Tyler shared with her what God was speaking. That led to a discussion that Tyler was not interested in six years of college! So, a few weeks later he was awakened (bored) at his desk in the Construction Tech class by a student runner who said the counselor said there was a man from Mt. Olive College there to recruit applicants and that he should talk with him. Tyler was persuaded that day where to attend.

Meanwhile, David and I were active in serving the youth and anywhere else there was a need at LBC. During this time, I saw his son increase in his awareness of the things of God, and he even made a profession of faith. But the boundaries demanded that we still maintain separate households. By this time in my spiritual life, I was aware of how my poor choices throughout life had affected my three children: the stress of living in crisis mode so often due to their father's behavior, to putting my work first and over-obligating as I served in the church, which led to more stress in a marriage. But what I did not see until time revealed was the positive impact of having a sincere zeal for the Lord and clinging to Him. Having a passion for Christ.

# CHAPTER FOUR

# Judah and Joseph United

Shane was the image of Judah gone away from the family to live in Canaan. For many reasons he was more comfortable calling another his family. During his late teenage years he was not blind to the things going on at home, and he began to come to me and tell me out of an effort to protect me. He always had a sense of needing to watch over us, including Tyler and Jessica. After completely exposing some actions of Jonathan, he could not understand why I would continue to stay with him. I would answer him that I have to listen to what the Lord is guiding me to do. He said, "It's like you are being beat up in the street and I come to your rescue and you turn on me!?" He was our bulldog and he took headship to watch out for us. No, Jessica did not have to worry about anyone in South Johnston mistreating her. And in our neighborhood we had some hateful neighbors. Reluctantly, when Tyler had enough of being threatened by some of the mean adults, he'd go get Shane. I did kind of enjoy having him fight my outside battles from time to time!

He returned during some very difficult times in his life and came to church with me in February of 2009. He shared that he wanted to be saved. That afternoon the Lord revealed to him his own sin, and he accepted Christ as his personal Savior. The miraculous thing about Shane's salvation is the thirst he had for the Word. I invited him to sit in on the Wednesday night bible study at our church the very next week. He said, "I feel like a baby in a college class." The next Saturday he went shopping for a new bible. I remember he called me twice from the store and spent about 2 hours shopping. Three weeks later, or exactly 21 days, he called me at midnight and said, "I'm finished." "Finished what?" I asked. "The bible. I just read the last verse in Revelation," he replied.

I was astonished. I knew he had a special purpose. But then I thought that he must have just grazed the top of it and not really understood what he read. So, I would come home and tell him about the message from my service (he was attending a different church). I wouldn't be able to finish the scene of the scripture referenced in our message before he would finish it for me. I took note that he was off the milk and had moved on to the meat of the Word. Within a short period of time, he was leading the youth, and the group was growing. All who knew him noticed the change.

It was Easter 2010 when Pastor Tim Bass mentioned that God had spoken to him about asking Tyler to preach a graduation message. Tyler experienced his first fears while preparing to stand and speak in front of men. God is so unique in the way He speaks to bring about His purposes. He used a church sign at the site of another church: "Whom do you fear?" The sign was there for two weeks, but the week before Tyler was to preach, in the midst of wrestling with fear, another line was added "God or man?" Tyler came to the conclusion that he had nothing to fear among those who loved him at this church. He gave a wonderful message to the church that day to "Move On" because a move of God is at hand. The Spirit is calling many to move for Him. Shane was there and confirmed the message, but he also affirmed that the words were not just directed to the graduates. Shane stood and proclaimed his call the very same day, to the very same group that Tyler had rallied support from two years prior. What is most special to me is the date was June 6th, my father's birthday. The truth stands in the scripture recorded in Proverbs 22:6, "Train up a child in the way he should go; and when he is old he will not depart from it." I received salvation and the grace of God when it pleased him to call me at the age of thirtyfive, with my oldest children already being in their early teens. It was not too late to live Deuteronomy 6:7, "And thou shalt teach them diligently unto thy children and shalt talk of them when thou sit at the table and when you walk about the way and when you lie down and rise up." Talk about what? The commandments and statutes of God in fear and reverence and love towards God.

Some folks don't like to hear about the Lord "all day long". I am hungry for the meat and thirsty for the living water that satisfies my soul daily like nothing else. Not satisfied to live off of leftovers but the daily Word that sustains us. There seems to be "a famine in the land" for His Word today. Despite all the disappointments and regrets in my life, I am rejoicing that my daughter is a delightful woman of God and that all my children have set high standards to live for God. I pray that their lives will be an example for this generation and continue training up the next.

# CHAPTER FIVE
# Moving on and Waiting

More difficult days were to follow those blessings as Tyler did "move on" the day after graduation. He set forth on his journey to Oak Island to serve at Camp Caswell. I was surprised by the pain I felt as my motherly duties seemed to be coming to an end. The feelings of severance were overwhelming as I looked ahead to move myself completely into my husband's house, thinking that I had served my last child through his youth and was now ready to turn my full affection to my husband. I moved myself, truly unwelcome, into a mission field that made me feel like I was in China-like the remake of the Karate Kid where the little boy is moved by his mother to live in China and no one likes him. By this time, David was so withdrawn, miserable to be with me, and unhappy with my priorities. The tension was so thick in the Sunday School class that we once shared. I would face the wall after teaching a lesson and hide my tears.

This was my world for the next year. Earlier, David had warned me that he would withdraw if I did not soon turn my attention to him. Apparently, I was too late on his terms. I had carried three beautiful roses at our wedding to represent God being in the center. I knew I had made mistakes towards him, and David had talked about the lack of guidance in the bible on how to merge two families. The closest examples in the bible were merging halfsiblings due to the man having more than one wife, and many times strife and envy followed. I had faith that Jesus could make all things new. I jumped at any biblical guidance I could find. I acted out the forty day devotion of the Love Dare and listened for marriage guidance on Focus on the Family. Now that I was feeling like no one needed me, I came to realize that my value in life seemed reliant on whom I could serve or help. I was back to those early days when I was a young teenage girl, often alone. I was created to be a helper. But the thought entered my head that no one needs me, but someone needs Jesus; keep seeking to serve.

Our friend Jan Tharrington Dorfer, former camp director of Stillwater Lodge in Meadow and administrator of our 2008 mission trip to Costa Rica, received a word for Tyler on the third day of his camp, and sent this scripture of encouragement from Habakkuk 2:24 concerning a vision: "Write the vision, and make it plain upon tables, that he may run that reads it. For the vision is yet for an appointed time, but at the end it shall speak and not lie: though it tarry, wait for it; because it will surely come, it will not tarry".

Tyler said his cafeteria duties were making it difficult to get to the "hatch time" to hear the guest speakers. However, this same night he received the message from Jan, he was determined to get there. He heard the closing remarks of a NFL player giving his testimony, and he stated "God will take you to difficult places to do great things." Tyler saw that the vision will bring many to salvation.

Tyler would text me feedback regularly when he would receive a word. "Did a devotion this morning from Romans

12. 'By the mercies of God present your bodies a living sacrifice, holy, acceptable unto God which is your reasonable service. And be not conformed to this world: but be ye transformed by the renewing of your mind, that ye may prove what is that good, acceptable, and perfect will of God'." This verse is vital after being born again: where are we to serve, how are we to serve, why are we to serve, and when is His timing for me to serve?

He texted me Philippians 2:1-11 after attending a small group meeting: "Let nothing be done in strife or vainglory, but in lowliness of mind let each esteem other better than themselves." I see a theme of being humble in your spirit as you serve. Apostle Paul spoke of a thorn in the flesh to the church of Corinth that afflicted him, "lest I should be exalted above measure through the abundance of the revelation." He will reveal more and more to you as you submit to hearing His direction.

*"Make a joyful noise unto the LORD all ye lands. Serve the LORD with gladness, come before his presence with singing. Know ye that the LORD he is God; it is he that made us, and not we ourselves; we are his people and the sheep of his pasture. Enter into His gates with thanksgiving and into his courts with praise: be thankful unto him, and bless his name. For the LORD is good; his mercies are everlasting and his* **truth** *endureth to all generations." Psalm 100*

*"I had fainted unless I had believed to see the goodness of the LORD in the land of the living. Wait on the LORD, be of good courage and he shall strengthen thine heart; wait, I say on the LORD." Psalm 27: 13,14*

My spiritual eyes were beginning to see the reality of the role my children would play in this era of time. They each have a special anointing as in each past generations to stand and live in truth for the benefit of our household and strangers as well. I felt in my spirit that there will be future persecution because those who stand for truth of the gospel are likely to be a target of evil. "And judgement is turned away backward and justice standeth afar off: for truth is fallen in the street, and equity cannot enter. Yea, truth faileth; and he that departeth from evil maketh himself a prey." Isaiah 59:13,14. Jesus said as he stood before Pilate accused of perverting the nation, "every one that is of the truth heareth my voice" (John 18:37). Jesus explained to Pilate that was the reason he was born was to bear witness to the truth. We have to be prepared to move with the gospel message and bear the truth "in season and out of season". Jesus is the Son of God and without Him there is no communion with the Father as noted in John 14:6. He is the only way. We cannot afford to turn from him no matter what pressures of persecution we will face.

It was prophesied by a complete stranger during a revival service in February of 2010, where Tyler and I were not known, that Tyler has a heart like King David and he will be used in miraculous ways. He also prophesied an expensive scholarship, not knowing Tyler's intent on Mount Olive, a private college. Truth! Anxious to see these events unfold, it was hard to wait. During the wait, the enemy was busy. My friend Jan was committed to pray for and support Tyler in his call from the day he stood up at the LBC annual business meeting in December of 2008 and read a verse of scripture. She knows about the painful attacks of the enemy that can occur within your own home and ministry. She shared with me about three occasions the devil spoke to her to keep her in despair as her camp ministry was under attack. She advised us: "I just told the enemy that I'm not even going to address you. You are not worthy. Only my God, the Most High, is worthy. He has already defeated you!"

During this first summer at Caswell, Tyler was content with not setting his own plans, but just following the Lord's lead from speaking to and praying for a homeless lady on the streets of Wilmington, to agreeing spontaneously to join in and teach a bible study lesson to a group of middle school girl campers!

Shane and I were enrolled to start the LBC satellite Theology course in Biblical Studies that August. A week later, Pastor J.D. Hudson asked Shane if he wanted to preach at a Sunday night service. His father Dan Hudson, the pastor of Garner Church of God, had asked him if he felt a call on his life to preach and offered to support him in any way. Two weeks prior at another church's revival, the pastor had prayed with Shane that the Lord would open up the opportunity for him to preach somewhere. We were eager to be in the classroom or any revival we heard going on. His first message at Garner was September 12, 2010. He preached on Romans 5 and a journey with Joseph having a dream. Over the next two months he preached about Jesus sending out two by two in Luke and being bold in our God through Thessalonians 3. Shane preached like a NASCAR driver coming out of the gate. Despite the fruit of his words he experienced a battlefield in his mind. These kinds of attacks can be overcome by recognizing that the devil distorts the truth of scripture, he is familiar with God's Word and will attempt to use it against you. Cast out any thoughts that do not line up with what is written. God has a plan for you despite what a man might interpret as well. One sure word we have been able to grab for confirmation is

Isaiah 49:18. "...The LORD has called me from the womb; from the bowels of my mother had he made mention of my name. And he had made my mouth like a sharp sword, in the shadow of his hand hath he hid me, and made me a polished shaft; in his quiver he hid me... And he said, It is a light thing that thou should be my servant to raise up the tribes of Jacob and to restore the preserved of Israel: I will also give thee as a light to the Gentiles..." Shane is a mouthpiece for the gospel. These are the words I chose to hold on to and use to encourage God's anointed. And I am so thankful for those who listened to the Spirit and supported him.

Even so, this was a hard summer for me as I was feeling like a stranger in David's home. I felt oppressed. I was busy, but I was running against some strong winds, and I felt the enemy wanted to keep me from soaring. During worship service, I felt prompted by the Spirit to get up and share something, but I was told by my husband that it is not scriptural for a woman to speak in church (written in 2 Timothy 2:11). As described in I Corinthians 11 concerning submission, ideally the man's headship is covered by Christ and the woman covered by the man. Man is the image and glory of God, and the woman is the glory of the man. Paul goes on to say in verse 17 that when giving this instruction, "I do not praise you because you came not together for the better but for the worse." Confusing instructions, but I could only apply it to myself. I suppose I was struggling with authority. This is hard to see when you are in the midst of the battle. When I wouldn't listen to David, he felt I didn't respect him. I was confused with what to do because I thought I should listen to the Spirit over the man.

Despite this oppression and confusion, I continued to serve in church and the community. I loved teaching the middle schoolaged children, "the Earthquakes", how to study God's Word. I kept pressing in the direction of sharing with young teens the truth of the gospel. I was also serving at the Pregnancy Crisis Center as a counselor to give hope, help, and strength to the ladies, and sometimes their partners, with the goal that they could make the right decisions in the face of the many lies from the Devil. In my ignorance, I had followed the lies. In these situations, Satan tempts all people to focus on themselves, their circumstances, and how their futures are ruined by an unexpected pregnancy. Given the opportunity, I was able to share the truth of God's Word with them and how the consequences of our decisions in life cause even more pain when we try to live apart from His instruction. His holy, inspired Word is written for our own protection, if only we would follow His Headship. As a nation we say it's a woman's choice, but we as a nation are perishing for lack of knowledge of the truth (Hosea 4:1).

I was given a dream as I awoke one morning of how our family could be together in ministry. David set up stages for the Department of Transportation. I dreamed of David setting up the stage on a tractor trailer bed for Shane to herald the gospel, Tyler down below healing, and Jessica praying and interceding with the hurting. The lost and saved are suffering and need to be ministered to with a message of hope whether it be hearing the good news of the gospel and receiving the message for the first time, or knowing you are saved and facing struggles from within your mind or from physical infirmities. I woke up thinking: Tyler has been gifted with musical instruments but who is going to sing? Little did I know, Jessica would marry Alex, who sings and plays guitar within their church. (Her future husband was right there with her as they worshipped together in the same church for three years. They began dating in 2012 and were wed June 1, 2013.) Yes, He has something for us to do if we are all willing.

In the meantime, God had placed Tyler at a college in the deserted city of Mount Olive. "Jesus went up to the mount of Olives" (John 8:1). He made a connection with Tyler Jernigan Ministries and met his good friend "Smooth". He had multiple opportunities for revival and worship. It seemed that Smooth was on the road four to five nights a week in revival, though I don't know how he did that with a college course load. "With God all things are possible" (Mark 10:27). God is pleased with the young people that are loving Him and living for Him. Tyler was given a second opportunity to preach at LBC on January 30, 2011. He spoke boldly with points of trust, obey, commit, confidence and surrender. Pastor Tim said he preached five sermons in one, and Tyler said that's what happens when he has so many months in between before having a chance to share. He was also blessed with a stipend through Gold Leaf Foundation which allowed him to do a leadership project with our youth pastor, Josh Williamson. They worked together to conduct a Boot Camp in May for the youth. We camped out in FEMA trailers on the church yard the whole weekend. Tyler preached that Sunday as well. Tyler and Ally had been dating one year at this time. I have to mention that I was very impressed with her sacrifice of spending her 19th birthday shut up at the church the entire weekend and sleeping in a trailer with a group of rowdy middle school girls who had no intention of sleeping at all. It was well worth it as we reaped three new converts and twelve decisions to grow in their walk with Christ. Tyler and Ally were growing in spiritual wisdom and understanding.

Meanwhile the tension was increasing at David's house. I believe David would agree this statement is true. I advise that if you marry unequally yoked in spiritual living and sacrifice, you will find yourselves going in different directions. I also advise to understand your partner's love language as outlined in Gary Chapman's book *The Five Love Languages*. We were not living in understanding of each other's language and were on opposite ends of the pole: doing acts of service versus a need for quality time. I'll admit I was way too busy and overcommitted in service. Regardless, to this day I pray blessings on his household. David had made up his mind that we could not get along and informed me he wanted me out of his house on Mother's Day 2011. Thank the Lord my house did not sell the prior year; I had an offer the first two weeks it was on the market, but the potential buyer changed his mind. The Lord knew I would need it. He knew the outcome from the beginning. Remember, I didn't take time to build an altar and ask Him, nor listen for a full answer. As I unloaded the last moving box from the truck, the first thing that came from my heart was "I want my name back." The Lord had spoken to me Matthew 10:14: "And whosoever shall not receive you, nor hear your words, when you depart out of that house or city, shake off the dust of your feet." In other words, keep your peace with you when you leave. Shane was standing there and said, "what name?" I said, "Franks". Then he replied "why not St. Pierre" and laughed. I was feeling the pain that I was not supposed to have made the move I did.

Tyler went off to his second year at Camp Caswell. We were allowed to visit him on Parent Weekend, but we made it an extended family trip with Jan, Ally, Jessica and his Dad. Jonathan was excited for the opportunity to support Tyler. Jan came prepared with a family devotion from a book *My Beautiful Broken Shell* by Carol H. Adams. The message portrays the image of shells that are lying on the beach, just as we all are, despite being pressed by the massive waves. The shell is broken, but not crushed, and still has a purpose. It is imperfect, but the beauty lies in what is left. The broken shell remains beautiful on the inside. Jonathan found a small conch shell on the beach that had an end that looked like an eye, and the base had been broken and left in the shape of an ear. He said, "Sometimes, you see, the Lord has to break you so you can hear." The atmosphere at the camp was so healing. It was amazing to see the young people pouring out their hearts to live in obedience to the Spirit and share their talents.

Tyler had the opportunity to preach outside of LBC this summer. One of his college classmates suggested to his father, the Pastor of Beulaville Baptist Church, that Tyler should preach for their Youth Sunday event. It was an awesome opportunity to step out a little more.

Shane got back in the pulpit on July 10th to preach on "A Call to Action". Praise God for Pastor Hudson continuing to call Shane to preach just when Shane would start doubting that he was useful in this manner. And praise God Shane was obedient and pressed through his thoughts each time Pastor called. Many from the church told me Shane was their motivator. His anointing was changing from being the out-of-the-gate preacher to the encourager. I told him I could see something different on his face that was not usually what I saw in him. There was a set smile while he spoke, a glow on his face, and a rhythmic movement in his posture and step.

Our friend Kim Schaller labeled him the "bouncing evangelist". I had the pleasure of participating in a ladies bible study with women from this church and it was a blessing to hear from them the anointing they saw on him. This group of ladies, Heidi, her sister Kelly Marshburn, Kim, Christina

Land, Renae Puckett, Lori Radford, Susan MacDonald, Stephanie Hammond and others have interceded and prayed fervently that the gospel would not to be hindered on any level. Moses had his brother Aaron and Hur to hold up his arms when the battle prevailed. As long as his arms were held up, God's people had victory over the enemy (Exodus 17:12). We are "Ladies of Hope" standing in the gap for each other.

Jessica was hired at Four Oaks Elementary out of college and taught fourth grade. The first year, her principal had her sign up to take classes for certification to teach Academically Gifted (AG) students. Jessica completed it but did not understand why she was asked to do that if she wasn't going to be used in that capacity. Into the third year of teaching, there were a whole lot of changes and Jessica became extremely stressed. She sought a way out and God provided just the solution. She had the opportunity to use her AG certification in Wilson. She worked and rested there for six months and acquired experience teaching Academically Gifted children. She always wanted to be in Wake County, and God provided a fulltime position at an elementary school. Jessica spent this year really searching out her special anointing of discernment. The Lord would go on to use her to send me in a new direction. She was also recognized for her steadfastness in her church and nominated by the homegroup to be deaconess. With her gift she has awareness of unwanted spirits and has identified the purpose for this gift is to intercede in prayer. She was also very sensitive to hearing the voice of God before she makes any moves.

**Mama, Jessica, Me**

Jessica watched Joyce Meyer preaching regularly, and I watched from time to time, so when Joyce was scheduled to be in Raleigh for a conference, we went along with several friends. As we were walking through the stadium, Jessica noticed a sign for medical missions and said "they need nurses, you should go." It was as if everything went into slow motion as the words came out of her mouth, guiding me straight from the throne. As you can see from my background, her gift of discernment did not come from my DNA makeup. I'm more like my mother who goes in to get an oil change and leaves with a new car. The last day of the conference, Joyce shared footage of "the Hand of Hope" in action. I could not stop crying. I was so moved with compassion. I applied online and looked over the projected trips thinking I would sign up for the closest and least expensive. On October 10, 2011, I received a reply for my acceptance to the team and was informed that Guatemala was filled, but would I consider Sri Lanka? "How long a flight is that? And by the way, where is it?" I sought advice from my friends and family about it. Jan said at first, "I know I'm not called to India, but you may be." Tyler said, "India? There will be other trips, Mom." Well, I knew who I needed to hear the confirmation from. I spent about four hours asking God to speak on this opportunity. I reviewed notes I had written back in 2008 when the ladies of LBC did the study "Living Life on Purpose" by Lysa Terkeurst. As I looked at my life purpose and the plans I had written, I saw "I am wife, mother, nurse, and teacher." Wife: on hold, mother: role has changed, teacher: not being used to lead bible study or youth group anymore. I am a nurse being called to missions! God gave me confirmation in this simple scripture from Proverbs 3:5: "Trust in God, lean not to your own understanding."

I joined the team to Sri Lanka not knowing a soul. I was so blessed to walk as a little dumb lamb just trusting in the Shepherd. The team was leaving JFK at 10 am to fly across the Indian Ocean, so I met Cyndi Stockton from California, and we stayed together overnight in a hotel before the long flight. At the airport, I took notice of all the team members arriving two by two many of us having arrived in the city the night before and roomed up. We were God's children. Soon we stepped into the Emirates, the largest airplane I've ever been in. The stewardess offered 7 different languages!

What impressed me the most was meeting the Christians of Sri Lanka. I was jet lagged the morning after we arrived, but I made my way ever so carefully across the street from the motel and sat in the open park there in Colombo. I had my bible in my hand, and a local man came bouncing my way. I thought "oh no, I'm by myself out here." He approached me to invite me to the conference on Friday. I said, "What conference?" He said, "have you not heard Joyce Meyer is coming here to this spot this Friday? I want you to come, and I want you to come to church with me this morning."

Wow, he put us saved people in America to shame with his boldness. Jareed and I spoke for a little while, and he shared with me his favorite scripture. Our conversation was limited because he didn't really understand my southern drawl, nor I his accent. Only 12-15% of the population are Christians, but they made it possible to set up the free clinics and volunteered alongside of us. I saw that the Holy Spirit is the same no matter the color of the skin. And every one of them cherish the Word and share their favorite scripture freely. It was a blessing to see the Hindu, Muslim, and Buddhists all sitting side by side as they waited, 800 people a day, to be served with love by the Christians. It was a monumental time in my life to say, "Here I am Lord, use me." I made lifelong connections with other Christians on this trip. Cyndi, my first roommate; Tania Arguello from Nevada, my roomie for the whole week; and Anna Rathnapala of Sri Lanka who volunteered one day with us. She still writes me to this day from Sri Lanka, she has no internet. Tania, Cyndi and I try to make it to St. Louis in September to Joyce's "Love Life" ladies conference as a mutual meeting place. And my family was blessed to connect with Tania at her house and arranged the best ski trip ever at Heavenly Ski Resort, Lake Tahoe. Cyndi was able to join us. The top of the ski mountain is on the California/Nevada state lines!

When we accept Jesus Christ based on faith, we receive power to be part of the Body of Christ to do marvelous works for the Kingdom. Do not limit yourself with your finite visions, but wait with expectation for what God wants to birth through you.

# CHAPTER SIX

## Beware of the Snares

Beware, you will have mountaintop experiences and leap for joy at the fullness of being a child of God, and then seemingly out of nowhere you find yourself in the flesh again. I brought back with me from Sri Lanka a physical host. And I was aware of a sense of spiritual principality surrounding me. Every night while in Sri Lanka I was awakened around 3 am, and I felt the Lord wanted me to read His Word for guidance for the team and upcoming day. But one night, midweek, I woke up with a very uncomfortable, dreadful feeling like my family needed me, but here I was on the other side of the world. Jonathan came to my mind and I thought how awful it would be if something happened to him, and Tyler had to deal with that alone. I'm not sure what that was all about, but I was unsettled.

The physical host came back with me due to not heeding the warning from the Spirit. I was raised on sweet tea. It became such an addiction that I would be in a panic when I traveled to Florida to see my Mom and north to Ohio to spend time with my cousin Debra (awesome Kingdom connections). My main concern was where I can get some good sweet tea, not that raspberry stuff. I would be very distracted and would cause my poor relatives such an inconvenience in trying to accommodate me. The Lord spoke to me on a prior mission to Hungary that this would be a problem. Not only was there no sweet tea there, but there was also no ice. I will say that the lesson for me in Hungary was to see that the pleasures and safety I had acquired in my home environment will not be accessible everywhere He takes me. Tyler and I were blessed to be a part of a mission to Hungary in 2009 with Pastor Scott Betts and his family. We were brought in to assist with an English Camp to teach English as a second language using the bible as the content. The bible I knew, but English... well let's just say they did not get their money's worth. While in Hungary, I was very distracted by my flesh's craving for my sugary drink at meal times. I remember getting so excited when I discovered a very small ice tray in the top of the refrigerator in the room we shared. I acted like I had discovered gold, "Tyler, look, it is an ice tray!! We don't have to drink our Fizz at room temperature!"

The Lord spoke to me concerning this issue again in August of 2011, just as He prepared me to go to Sri Lanka. I gave up the tea for good so that I would not waste precious time there looking to meet this desire. But the compromise came on the very last day of the trip. Our leaders Ashley and Wade had cautioned us on the do's and don'ts of the dietary list. No ice, no fountain drinks, and nothing that has to be washed in water, like lettuce. We had a two hour shopping spree on Saturday and got our food on the run. I won't mention the name of the food chain, but yes, they are worldwide. I began to get a thought of how hard I had worked and how I would love to have a soda. I could order the cardboard chicken nuggets, but I just wanted to treat myself to the sugar energy. Ashley asked and discovered that their water was distilled. With that, she advised that it should be safe, but to get it without the ice just in case. This is where the host got into my system. I was able to hold back the nausea, barely, until we boarded the plane, but I pitied the young man from Amsterdam who was assigned to sit beside me for the next five hours as we traveled from Colombo to Dubai. I say the Lord did watch out for me by having me on the last row so that when I turned my head in sickness no one was back there. And the young man was so kind to let me have his bag and extra blankets as he nursed me. I told him I was with a team of thirty nurses on this plane, but he was the unlucky one to be with me.

Once home, I started waking up between 2-3am every night with hot flashes, but also began having them throughout the day. I would feel a hot flush come over me and I would get short-tempered; I even snapped at my manager. I decided I should go and explain my behavior to Ellen Wheaton, my manager. She is a Christian, and I have been blessed to have her authority over me. We could talk on a spiritual level. I have been in her office before and she has taken my feet in her hands and prayed for healing of my plantar fascitis. I have endured a few physical challenges related to my years of nursing, and Ellen has prayed with me many times. I spoke with Ellen about possible hormone imbalances, but wondered why the symptoms of menopause would come on suddenly. I announced that God's grace was sufficient for me and I could endure the physical attacks. That is what Apostle Paul said concerning his thorn in the flesh. That night I slept through the night and have never been bothered again with the hot flashes as a result of my profession of faith in an awesome God. One snare that I need to continue to work on in my spiritual formation and process of sanctification is my behavior under stress.

I have the power to react differently. It is a choice to snap or not. That is a whole separate testimony and a work in progress. Despite our surroundings and circumstances, we can speak peace regardless of the physical attacks or perceived environment.

Jessica encountered some financial pressures when she moved back from Wilson and took the job in Wake County as I mentioned earlier. She wanted to live alone on her own, but this would prove to be a financial challenge. During this time in her life, she was really seeking to understand her spiritual gifts and grow in them. The Lord spoke to her in prayer "this is not what I had for you." The Lord blessed her right out of there and right on time as the pressures mounted financially. She found someone to sublease the remaining few months of the contract, a generous friend allowed her to stay with her for a time, and then shortly thereafter He opened up to her an opportunity to live affordably in the lower level of a widow's home for the next year until she married Alex.

During Tyler's sophomore year at Mt. Olive he became unsatisfied with the leadership role he had taken as a Resident Advisor in his dorm. He was just not a good fit for the job. He was not allowed to leave the building over the weekends because he was on call. He was not happy with the amount of coverage that fell on the holidays and Spring Break. He was miserable, and I could sense the changes in his personality. During these few short weeks, he made some unwise decisions on the campus that could have left a bad scar on his name and character. Mrs. Wilson, my brother Stuart's mother-in-law and my spiritual mother, had called me about some other issues one day, and as we were talking her tone of voice changed as if the Spirit were speaking to her, and she asked, "Lisa, is there anything I can pray for you about?" I said, "Yes, let us pray for Tyler." That is all I told her. She called me back two days later and said, "Lisa, the Lord has said Tyler has reached an impasse." Another week passed and she called back and added, "The Lord said, the enemy meant this as an attack against his soul, this is no childish play."

In the midst of the anguish over the circumstances, Tyler was sitting in one of his business classes and the professor was explaining how unions function. He said, "When two businesses can't come to an agreement, they have reached an impasse and they must have a mediator to act as a go between." Tyler was facing some serious accusations on campus. Christ was assuring Tyler with these references that He would fight the battle, but that Tyler must form his alliance with His Sovereign Lord. When Christ is your advocate, case dismissed.

Shane continued to submit to the pastor's calls to preach when he was contacted. Shane had first preached the story of Joseph who had a dream and how the enemy of Joseph's soul used the envy of his brothers to keep him under enslavement. God allowed these attacks on Joseph so that he would be in his appointed place to later help his family, along with many others, to survive during the famine and to preserve their souls. It was because of Judah's petition for Joseph that he was not killed, and then later Judah would stand in the gap to persuade their father Jacob to let them travel to Egypt where they would be saved and reunited. I know Shane has souls appointed to him. The enemy would love to have him think his dreams were over. After much prayer and desire to have a partner in this journey of life, the Lord answered our prayer and revealed Shane's lovely help mate (Gen 2:18), Stacie.

*"For I consider that the sufferings of this present time are not worthy to be compared with the glory that is to be revealed to us. For the anxious longing for the creation waits eagerly for the revealing to the sons of God. For the creation was subjected to futility, not willingly but because of Him who subjected it, in hope that the creation itself also will be set free from its slavery to corruption into the freedom of the glory of the children of God. For we know that the whole creation groans and suffers the pains of childbirth together until now. And not only this, but also we ourselves, having the first fruits of the Spirit, even we ourselves groan within ourselves, waiting eagerly for our adoption as sons, the redemption of our body. For in hope we have been saved, but hope that is seen is not hope; for who hopes for what he already sees? But if we hope for what we do not see, with perseverance we wait eagerly for it. In the same way the Spirit also helps our weakness; for we do not know how to pray as we should, but the Spirit Himself intercedes for us with groanings too deep for words; and He who searches the hearts knows what the mind of the Spirit is, because He intercedes for the saints according to the will of God." (Romans 8:18-27 NASB)*

The enemy of our soul uses various distractions in attempts to hinder, which can affect how you choose to do the "good and acceptable" and miss out on the perfect will of the Father. Despite which strategies the enemy uses to distort the view of your circumstance, God has a plan for our good for those who love him and "who are the called according to his purpose." (Romans 8:28)

# CHAPTER SEVEN

# "A Sweet smelling Savour"

Jessica attends a church in Raleigh that is a plant of a larger church. The average age of the congregation is around thirtyfive. The atmosphere is very casual, and everyone walks around with coffee cups in their hands drinking coffee throughout the service. I said to Jessica, "I sure hope God likes the smell of coffee, because I sure do not." I was talking to Shane about it and said, "You know, most churches today have coffee brewing in the atmosphere and I hate the smell of coffee. I sure hope God is pleased with it." Shane said, "What is a sweet smell to the LORD?" I thought about all the animal sacrifices that had to be made on a daily basis for atonement during the time of the Old Testament, and I was under the impression that God liked the smell of meat roasting, particularly the fat. Also, incense was offered on the golden altar in the holy place as a sweet aroma. Shane said, "our praise is like a sweet smell to Him." "The fruit of our lips giving thanks to His name" (Hebrews 13:15). The law required the priest to intercede on behalf of the one bringing the offering, with specific instructions for preparation depending on the type of offering being made. But the one receiving atonement brought praise to God along with their sacrifice. We can learn from King Saul's mistake: "It is better to obey His voice than to sacrifice, and to hearken than the fat of rams" (1 Samuel 15:22).

I was blessed to be a part of the Hand of Hope team in Guatemala in 2013. Our leader, Laura, asked for volunteers to give morning devotions prior to setting out for the day. I asked the Lord, "Is there anything I should be sharing?" The word sacrifice came to me. I thought about how we all had made some sort of sacrifice to be away from home for a week to serve together. We were complete strangers to one another (except Tania was on this trip with me), traveling from all four corners of the world to glorify God and I praise him for the opportunity. I shared the eye-opening word received from that conversation with Shane that we who are stuck in our religious traditions of worship should be receptive to change. We shouldn't be so upset with the changes the new generation is bringing, as long as what they are offering brings Him praise.

Hebrews 13:10-12 says "We have an altar, whereof they have no right to eat which serve the tabernacle. For the bodies of those beasts, whose blood is brought into the sanctuary by the high priest for sin, are burned without the camp. Wherefore Jesus also that he might sanctify the people with his own blood, suffered without the gate. Let us go forth therefore unto him without the camp, bearing his reproach." Verses 20 and 21: "Now the God of peace, that brought again from the dead our Lord Jesus that great shepherd of the sheep, through the blood of the everlasting covenant, make you perfect in every good work to do his will, working in you that which is well-pleasing in his sight, through Jesus Christ: to whom be glory for ever and ever." Jesus was the ultimate sacrifice given once and for all. King David wrote prophetically of the Messiah to come in Psalm 22:8, "He trusted on the LORD that he would deliver him: let him deliver him, seeing he delighted in him." Peter wrote in his first epistle in chapter 4:11, "If any man speak, let him speak as the oracles of God; if any man minister, let him do it as of the ability which God gives, that God in all things may be glorified through Jesus Christ, to whom be praise and dominion for ever and ever." Apostle Paul encouraged the Ephesians to be followers of God and walk in love, as Christ also loved us and gave himself as a offering and sacrifice to God for a "sweet smelling savour" (Ephesians 5:2). It is pleasing to the Father God when we give continual praise to His son and live according to God in the spirit. And He will delight in you.

# CHAPTER EIGHT

# The Love of God

While in Guatemala, my heart was filled with so much compassion for the things I saw. We served the scavengers who survived for generations off a garbage dump site in the outskirts of Guatemala City. We set up a medical clinic to offer free treatment for their physical needs. This time I volunteered in the ministry area. While the clients waited for their drug prescriptions, we asked how we could pray for their spiritual needs. Many had a profession of Christ, others a knowledge of him, and some who did not know of Jesus were open to hearing and receiving. As I listened to their needs, I was not surprised that they might would waver in their faith. Destitute living conditions. Crime had few impediments, and a person's life seemed to have no value since people freely murdered without consequences in their community. Gangs were rampant in order to survive. The common request was to pray for "la familia." Mothers grieved over their teenage sons' senseless murders over jealousy or to gain a possession. One squatter told me his neighbors were threatening to take his little home he had built from scraps twenty-five years ago. He is single and works all day in the garbage, and the neighboring squatters do not think he needs it as much as they. Others had voiced concerns over violence from being in such a cramped space with their neighbors.

Many of us on the team were feeling like we had so much and we would just love to give them a portion of our own belongings. After the first day of this exposure and being exhausted from daylong prayer, Lyn Rachez suggested we meet and worship to be refueled. That night, Lyn suggested we ask God to speak to our hearts about our questions and thoughts. As we meditated in prayer to enter into the holiest of communion through worship, I asked God, "Why do your children, who profess Jesus as Lord, have such a variation of provision in this life here on earth?" I felt that I was in a sea with thousands of people as I meditated in worship. I had my arms stretched out to my sides. I began to feel a burning pressure in the palms of my hands. I told the Lord that I had wanted so badly to reach in my fanny pack and give the young woman I prayed with the money I had with me. She had to miss working in the garbage dump for two days because her baby was sick, and she had come seeking help for this child, her youngest of four children. Five dollars would have changed her situation. However, we had been instructed not to hand out money, so I prayed the Lord would provide for her needs and that she would find something of value on the way back home. He let me know what I could do was so limited, but He would take care of it all, every one of his children. He paid it on the cross. He let me know he sees all the needs. We know compassion is an attribute of Christ. His Word states "But when he saw the multitudes, he was moved with compassion on them..." (Matthew 9:36). Because God's spirit lives in me, I felt the same.

I was sharing with Shane how the mission had impacted me. I felt grieved by the reality of the deep levels of suffering I witnessed. Shane interjected that we should be filled with the same level of compassion in our everyday lives, not just during a limited time we have set aside to give of ourselves in a certain destination. He preached a message to edify and exhort the church to show compassion daily, everywhere and anywhere we have the opportunity.

The Spirit works in unity as He stirs His people in a common area. I have seen Tyler and Shane preach very similar messages, as they were often asked to preach at parallel times in two different places, even though they had not discussed with each other what God was speaking to them. So at the same time Shane was preaching compassion, Tyler was lead to preach on God's love. "God so loved the world that he gave His only begotten son..." (John 3:16). The everlasting love of the Father does have one condition, and that is to believe. Jesus did not come to condemn, but to save. God's love does not have only a past tense. As He loved, He gave. He gave despite your position of allegiance at the time. Jesus' life was a gift that keeps on giving. Jesus suffered for mankind despite his own people, the Israelites' lack of allegiance at the time. The Holy Triune remain in love with you despite the position you take or the choices you make. I remember talking with my Daddy when it appeared that Jonathan was on the mend from the troubles in his life back in 2003, I said to my Dad, "Isn't this great, this is what I've been longing for?!" His reply: "I don't know, I haven't seen the end of the story yet." However, God the Father does know the end of the story for each one of us. There is always grace and mercy to repent and turn back to the Holy Father. As long as there is breath, there is hope. The character of the Holy Father speaks repentance, restoration, and relationship. I know God spoke to me on our family visit to see Tyler that summer at Caswell concerning Jonathan from 2 Corinthians 2:6-8 "Sufficient to such a man is this punishment, which was inflicted of many. So that contrariwise ye ought rather to forgive him, and comfort him, lest perhaps such a one should be swallowed up with much sorrow. Wherefore I beseech you that ye would confirm your love toward him." This verse is a followup to the message in the first letter to the Corinthians in chapter 5 which states to put the person out from among you as I was led to do in separating but then He guides that soul toward restoration. That is the heart of God. However, man is still free to serve whom he will but is only liberated when one submits the whole heart to Him.

As Tyler was spiritually lead, he gave a comparative illustration of how God created Adam and saw that it was not good for man to be alone. He created Eve from the side of man to become a companion for him. The woman represents additional attributes of God's character, that of a helper. God created each one of us before we were even in our mother's womb. He wants us to chose Him, to journey relationally with Him, and to give us the helper of the Holy Spirit to bring comfort to our weary lives and to keep us in the joy of our hope. I remember making this point several times to the Guatemalans who professed knowing Christ. I exhorted them to be aware that we should not neglect this relationship. We wouldn't get up each morning and go through the day without speaking to our husband, parents, or children. If we conducted ourselves solo, leaving our family out, they would probably not stay around very long. Fortunately, God is longsuffering, and he patiently waits for our affection.

He will use you to show His love to others. It was December 2011, a very cold day. I was driving to a local store, and as I came to a busy stoplight off an exit from the highway, I saw a man standing and holding a cardboard sign. As I drove past, everything went into slow motion, and I noticed his right arm was in the dirtiest cast I had ever seen. The Spirit of the Lord spoke to me and asked, "Are you going to pass by on the other side?" So I went to the next light, did a U-turn, parked nearby, and walked to where he was standing. I spoke with Randy about 45 minutes and learned he had no teeth, heart disease, and had been sleeping in a tent. His pants were torn and I saw his long john coming through. I was freezing just standing there during that time, and he had been standing out there all day. I asked if I could pray with him that his circumstances would change. He graciously removed his ball cap and we prayed "to the blood of the Lamb, Jesus" as he said. He was raised in a Christian home and was very proud of his heritage from his grandmother and mother. His choices in life left him on the outskirts so he was unwelcome to go visit his mother.

I would often look for Randy in this spot and another that he frequented. I would stop and talk to him and encourage him. I wanted to help him get back into the Bible and glean some hope from how the Father would welcome Him back and turn everything around. We began to meet on Sunday afternoons, mostly at the local gas station where we could sit down for an hour or so. He told me he had applied for disability and had been turned down twice, but he was hopeful that he would qualify at his next hearing. I was cautious as a female, and I realized it would be better if a man would join us. Tyler and Ally stopped and introduced themselves, and Randy later met Shane. I was trying to convince him to come to church with me at LBC on Sunday morning, but he felt that he wouldn't be dressed properly. Towards the end of the summer, I was shocked to see that one of our men in the church had picked Randy up and brought him in. Tyler was serving as Youth Pastor at East Erwin Baptist Church. I soon learned that Randy's mother not only lived near the church, but also attended the same church with Tyler. What are the odds?

I saw Randy was growing more weary and troubled with his living arrangements. At this point, he was living in a house with several others, and as long as he could bring home $10 a day, he could stay there. He told me that he had a hearing date for his disability claim at the end of September. I began to ponder in my heart the idea of him staying with us a few days until the hearing. I talked with Tyler about it, and after bible study that Sunday, I brought him home. Wednesday we went to the hearing, but I learned that decisions are not made right away and it could take months. Oh well, I had not considered that! I thought he would get a check that day and off we would go to find living arrangements for him. Fortunately, it was the end of the fiscal year, so he was approved within a week and received a check within a month. My neighbors, the Bolton's and the Hansen's were supportive of him. Jessica and Alex embraced him as well. Life drastically changed when he got his money. I noticed behavior changes, and I was not pleased. Tyler and I were home together, and I did not know, but Tyler was fasting to hear a solution for this situation.

We were cleaning up the back yard of trees that had recently been cut down and taking huge loads to the county dump site. When we came inside the house throughout the day we would notice that Randy was still in his room. Finally, as we came in for the night, I told Tyler that we should check on him. I opened the door and immediately began CPR. Tyler called 911 and he left in an ambulance. He was admitted to the hospital I work at, and after being on a ventilator for 3-4 days he made a full recovery. Oddly, his older brother was also in the hospital on the same floor just down the hall. I let it be known that Randy would not be coming back to my house, but during this week his brother died. The mother, Faith, was making the arrangements for the funeral to be held at their church, so, out of empathy we let him come home with us to stay until the funeral. As he walked in the door of our home, he said, "I have never known such love from a family that doesn't even know me." I think we achieved God's purpose.

# CHAPTER NINE

# Family

I stated in the beginning that I am thankful for my Christian family line. God designed the family for love, support, unity, and a sense of belonging. The Levites were the sons, or tribe, of Israel designated for priestly duty, to intercede for the people and to make atonement for their sins so that they could be acceptable to God. The book of Matthew introduces the lineage of the generations to Jesus Christ, the spotless lamb given once and for all to make atonement for the people. Jesus is the high priest of the heavenly tabernacle today. The priests appointed to serve here on earth were just a foreshadow of what was to come. Jesus was not born into the inheritance of a Levitical priest, but he is the mediator of a better covenant. Matthew was written to the Hebrews to show them the lineage of Jesus that goes all the way back to Father Abraham, from whom all nations would be blessed. And they would also see the blood line to the famous King David through the tribe of Judah, the fourth son of Israel. God set up the authority of a king over the people because they wanted to be like all the other nations. They did not understand the authority of Jesus as King, because it did not look like what they had known. "But some said, Shall Christ come out of Galilee? (John 7:41). I want to leave written encouragement for my family of Gentiles on how we can be grafted into that green olive tree (Jeremiah 11:16). Historically recorded in Matthew, you will find records of Gentile women who wanted the God of the Hebrews so much that they were considered righteous by their faith, and therefore entered into the lineage. The only one who can intercede to bring us into this righteous blood line is Jesus, our High Priest. And this eternal gift of inheritance comes by faith. "But as many as received him, to them gave he power to become the sons of God, even to them that believe on his name" (John 1:12).

My cousin, Gus, called himself an enigma. When God created him and the trials he would encounter, He threw away the mold, he explained. Gus had his share of challenges for sure. His father, Ralph Keel, at the age of 44 was murdered, and his mother died one year later. Thirteen-year-old Gus and his younger brother, Mickey, became orphans.

He shared with me how his parents took him to church faithfully every Sunday. He said he never missed a Sunday in seven years of his youth. His parents' obedience to raising their children up in the admonition of the Lord had lead Gus to share with me that he knew his Savior. He was at peace as he faced the fact that his body was failing. After eleven years under treatment at Duke Medical Center, known for its research, no diagnosis or cure was ever found. At the young age of 49, Gus was content in the knowledge that his soul would leave his mortal body; leaving a body destined to corruption, but to be given a glorified body which is incorruptible in the presence of our Heavenly Father.

Dr. Gus Keel knew at the age of three he wanted to be a "doggie doctor". He prevailed and reached his goal despite his circumstances. He was known to get along better with animals than some people. His sense of humor might have left you questioning his character, but I know he has used laughter as a relief in life, and he will have a special "comedy cloud" in heaven. As his physical frame shrank in ways, his heart shined through in larger ways as he pleaded with his closest loved ones to please "allow Jesus into your heart." He told me that one of his biggest fears of dying was not having assurance that all will be together for eternity. I noticed that Gus never pleaded with God to be healed to extend his time. He told my Aunt Alice and the cousins living close to him not to take him to the hospital anymore. He asked them to just sit with him while he died. He told me his blood pressure had been dropping low and would cause him to pass out for hours at a time. The family went to check on him and found him in his recliner chair, pale, pulseless, and not breathing for half an hour. They did not know what to do; they felt helpless. They witnessed his dog, Flossie, suddenly make an unusual howl towards heaven.

She proceeded to run and jumped on Gus, licked his face, and he aroused. Flossie interceded on his behalf. He was able to work until the author and finisher of his faith said it was time to go home. He was blessed to have one last hunting trip that was televised with Roger Raglin. One month later he peacefully left us on October 24, 2013. Gus had said, "I hope Mama and Daddy don't mind that I'm going to run and see my dogs first!"

Jesus has gone before us to prepare a place for us. In his home are many mansions. Clearly, Jesus is the way. The truth is He is the only way to this heavenly home. I urge my family, those who are alive today and those in the future generations, to clean out those rooms in your heart that are sinful by nature. And it is not enough to be "cleaned up", but you have to fill those places with more of Jesus. If you are searching your heart now and saying, "I'm a good person, I live a good life and have not made bad choices or been in bad circumstances," then you need to recognize those thoughts as pride. Pride is what got Lucifer evicted from heaven. Let's go back to the first Adam. His and Eve's eyes were opened when they took the fruit of the tree of the knowledge of good and evil. "When the woman saw that the tree was good for food, and that it was pleasant to the eyes, and a tree to be desired to make one wise, she took of the fruit thereof, and did eat, and gave also unto her husband with her and he did eat" (Genesis 3:6). Eve was tempted by her physical senses and the pride of knowing what God knows. Now that we have knowledge of good and evil, we have to make a choice. We cannot remain blind in our sinful nature. Choose good; choose life for eternity. Jesus chose to leave heaven so he could take that curse of knowing evil upon himself and nail it to a tree once and for all.

I thank God for my dad, James H. Keel (June 6, 1932 January 14, 2003). He was the most cheerful person I have ever known. Anyone who knew him would agree. He had retired and was able to enjoy things he liked to do for seventeen years, until the night he urinated blood and ended up in an emergency room at an outlying hospital. They gave him no hope of surviving the kidney mass. It was so large that they could not even recommend a possible intervention. By God's grace, he went to Duke Medical Center, and they did remove the kidney. They gave us another eighteen months to hear him humbly talk about the Lord. Daddy came to know at the end of his days who "possessed his reins" (Psalm 139:13). He had, to an extent, lived doing what he pleased, but there was no place he could go that he could flee from His presence. I am very thankful that in his last days he had a very loving companion named Betty, who stayed by his side through the tough times of his failing condition.

It was hard times for me because near the end of 2002, at the same time Daddy had a recurrence of cancer and brain surgery that lead to many complications, Teddy and Timmy were in the car accident. Timmy died within twenty four hours of the accident, before Shane, Jessica, their Aunt Liz, and myself could get to Connecticut. Timmy was buried on Jessica's eighteenth birthday. Teddy lived for three more weeks, but died the day after Shane's nineteenth birthday and was buried on New Year's Eve. About two weeks later, my Dad passed and was buried around Tyler's eleventh birthday. There was heavy grief to overcome in the St. Pierre and Keel family. It is hard to be separated from their physical existence, but we have a second coming to hope for in Jesus. Jesus fulfilled the Passover meal at the Last Supper, and then he displayed the power of the resurrection. He was the first fruits of that power, and because of Him we can have hope in the resurrection of our spirits at His Second Coming. If Jesus is Lord of our life, then we will ALL sit and share another meal together; no more to be separated.

A Poem of Thanksgiving: Happy Father's Day 2002
Dear Heavenly Father,
I'd like to thank you for providing me,
with the best earthly father there could be.
He persevered when things went wrong,
he kept his head up to remain strong.
It appeared unfair for a man alone,
to raise his children and provide a home.
My Daddy never failed to provide security,
within the home there was unity.

He was always pleasant with a smile,
I could count on him to go the extra mile.
He helped me in times of trouble,
my burdens he lightened before they doubled.
We could reason together; he was always fair;
I knew he would be there.
Thank you Lord for saving his soul;
despite his physical changes, his spirit remains whole.
It gives joy and peace to me
that we will live in your Kingdom for eternity.

**Me and Daddy**

My Daddy lived to see his oldest grandson Shane graduate from high school. He would have never dreamed that ten years later Shane would preach to the 2013 graduates of his church with the focus on "now it is your turn". Just as God called Moses and parted the Red Sea, he led them out of bondage into victory. He parted the Jordan to give them the promised land, and He moved the enemy aside, battle after battle. It is our turn for Him to speak to us. There are conditions to receiving victory. We have to completely submit our lives to Him. When we try to mark our own paths or grumble that it was better "back when" (listen church, as the Spirit says), we will keep wandering in the wilderness and lose the small battles we thought we could handle. The Israelites did so after the big victory over the city of Jericho; they lost the small battle of Ai when they approached it their own way. God did give them rest from their enemies. As Joshua grew old, he encouraged God's people "that ye turn not aside therefrom to the right hand or to the left...but cleave unto the Lord your God..." (Joshua 23:6,8). "Now therefore fear the LORD, and serve him in sincerity and in truth: and put away the gods which your fathers served on the other side of the flood, and in Egypt and serve ye the LORD. And if it seem evil unto you to serve the LORD, choose ye this day whom ye will serve..." (Joshua 24:14,15).

Despite what your battle looks like, let us remember what David did in his Ziklag experience as his own people momentarily turned against him; he encouraged himself in the LORD our God (1 Samuel 30:6). Wouldn't you rather "tarry by the stuff" and live in the power that comes from being a child of God that which is given to all who believe? Jesus said, "...He that believes on me and the works that I do, shall he do also, and greater works than these shall he do..." (John 14:12).

I encourage you readers to love Him, keep His commandments and abide in the Vine.

*Grandpa Keel, Tyler, Shane, Jessica*

*Shane and Grandpa Keel*

**Me, Alan, Stuart**

**Alan, Me, Stuart**

# Reference

1. Crosby, Franny J., and Phoebe P. Knapp. *Blessed Assurance*. 1873.

2. In His Wakes is a nonprofit ministry that uses water sports to share the love of Christ. Founded by Kristi Overton Johnson.

3. Hand of Hope is the missions arm of Joyce Meyer Ministries to help hurting people and alleviate human suffering.

4. Terkeurst, Lysa. *Living Life on Purpose*. A ministry of Moody Bible Institute. 2000

5. Chapman, Gary. *The Five Love Languages: How to Express Heartfelt Commitment to Your Mate"*. Moody Press. 1995

6. Alex and Stephen Kendrick. *The Love Dare*. B&H Publishing Group. 2008

7. Roger Raglin is a hunter producing hunting videos on the Outdoor Channel.

8. Hall, Elvina. *Jesus Paid it All*. 1865. Stanfill, Kristian. 2015

Printed in the United States
by Baker & Taylor Publisher Services